# RECIPE JOURNAL

First published in 2018 by Erin Rose Publishing



Design: Julie Anson

ISBN: 978-1-911492-43-6

A CIP record for this book is available from the British Library.

# CONTENTS

| RECIPE NAME | PAGE | RECIPE NAME | PAGE |
|---|---|---|---|
| ....................... | ....... | ....................... | ....... |
| ....................... | ....... | ....................... | ....... |
| ....................... | ....... | ....................... | ....... |
| ....................... | ....... | ....................... | ....... |
| ....................... | ....... | ....................... | ....... |
| ....................... | ....... | ....................... | ....... |
| ....................... | ....... | ....................... | ....... |
| ....................... | ....... | ....................... | ....... |
| ....................... | ....... | ....................... | ....... |
| ....................... | ....... | ....................... | ....... |
| ....................... | ....... | ....................... | ....... |
| ....................... | ....... | ....................... | ....... |
| ....................... | ....... | ....................... | ....... |
| ....................... | ....... | ....................... | ....... |
| ....................... | ....... | ....................... | ....... |
| ....................... | ....... | ....................... | ....... |
| ....................... | ....... | ....................... | ....... |

# CONTENTS

| RECIPE NAME | PAGE | RECIPE NAME | PAGE |
|---|---|---|---|

# CONTENTS

| RECIPE NAME | PAGE | RECIPE NAME | PAGE |
|---|---|---|---|

# MEASURES & TEMPERATURE CONVERSION CHART

## DRY INGREDIENTS

| | | | |
|---|---|---|---|
| ¼oz | 7g | 8oz | 225g |
| ½oz | 15g | 9oz | 250g |
| ¾oz | 20g | 11oz | 300g |
| 1oz | 25g | 10oz | 275g |
| 1½oz | 40g | 12oz | 350g |
| 2oz | 50g | 1lb | 450g |
| 2½oz | 60g | 1½lb | 675g |
| 3oz | 75g | 2lb | 900g |
| 4oz | 125g | 3lb | 1.35kg |
| 5oz | 150g | 4lb | 1.8kg |
| 6oz | 175g | 4½lb | 2kg |
| 7oz | 200g | 5lb | 2.25kg |

## LIQUID INGREDIENTS

| | | | |
|---|---|---|---|
| 1fl oz | 25mls | 14fl oz | 400mls |
| 2fl oz | 50mls | 15fl oz | 450mls |
| 3fl oz | 75mls | 1 pint | 600mls |
| 3½ fl oz | 100mls | 1¼ pints | 750mls |
| 4fl oz | 125mls | 1½ pints | 1 litre |
| 5fl oz | 150mls | | |
| 6fl oz | 175mls | | |
| 7fl oz | 200mls | | |
| 8fl oz | 250mls | | |
| ½ pint | 300mls | | |
| 12fl oz | 360mls | | |

## TEMPERATURE

| Gas Mark | F | C |
|---|---|---|
| 1 | 275°F | 140°C |
| 2 | 300°F | 150°C |
| 3 | 325°F | 170°C |
| 4 | 350°F | 180°C |
| 5 | 375°F | 190°C |
| 6 | 400°F | 200°C |
| 7 | 425°F | 220°C |
| 8 | 450°F | 230°C |
| 9 | 475°F | 240°C |

## RECIPE FOR



Prep Time ......... Cooking Time ......... Temp. ......... Serves.........

### INGREDIENTS

### METHOD

### NOTES

# RECIPE FOR

Prep Time ......... Cooking Time ......... Temp. ......... Serves. .........

## INGREDIENTS

.......................... .......................... ..........................

.......................... .......................... ..........................

.......................... .......................... ..........................

.......................... .......................... ..........................

.......................... .......................... ..........................

.......................... .......................... ..........................

## METHOD

..................................................................................

..................................................................................

..................................................................................

..................................................................................

..................................................................................

..................................................................................

..................................................................................

..................................................................................

..................................................................................

..................................................................................

..................................................................................

..................................................................................

..................................................................................

## NOTES

..................................................................................

..................................................................................

..................................................................................

# RECIPE FOR

Prep Time ......... Cooking Time ......... Temp. ......... Serves. .........

## INGREDIENTS

## METHOD

## NOTES

# RECIPE FOR

Prep Time ......... Cooking Time ......... Temp. ......... Serves. .........

## INGREDIENTS

## METHOD

## NOTES

# RECIPE FOR

Prep Time ......... Cooking Time ......... Temp. ......... Serves. .........

## INGREDIENTS

## METHOD

## NOTES

# RECIPE FOR

Prep Time ......... Cooking Time ......... Temp. ......... Serves. .........

## INGREDIENTS

## METHOD

## NOTES

# RECIPE FOR

Prep Time ......... Cooking Time ......... Temp. ......... Serves. .........

## INGREDIENTS

## METHOD

## NOTES

# RECIPE FOR

Prep Time ......... Cooking Time ......... Temp. ......... Serves. .........

## INGREDIENTS

## METHOD

## NOTES

# RECIPE FOR

Prep Time ......... Cooking Time ......... Temp. ......... Serves.........

## INGREDIENTS

## METHOD

## NOTES

# RECIPE FOR

Prep Time ......... Cooking Time ......... Temp. ......... Serves. .........

## INGREDIENTS

## METHOD

## NOTES

# RECIPE FOR

Prep Time ......... Cooking Time ......... Temp ......... Serves.........

## INGREDIENTS

## METHOD

## NOTES

# RECIPE FOR

Prep Time ......... Cooking Time ......... Temp.......... Serves.........

## INGREDIENTS

## METHOD

## NOTES

# RECIPE FOR

Prep Time ......... Cooking Time ......... Temp. ......... Serves.........

## INGREDIENTS

## METHOD

## NOTES

# RECIPE FOR

Prep Time ......... Cooking Time ......... Temp. ......... Serves. .........

## INGREDIENTS

## METHOD

## NOTES

# RECIPE FOR

Prep Time ......... Cooking Time ......... Temp. ......... Serves.........

## INGREDIENTS

## METHOD

## NOTES

# RECIPE FOR

Prep Time ......... Cooking Time ......... Temp. ......... Serves.........

## INGREDIENTS

## METHOD

## NOTES

# RECIPE FOR

Prep Time ......... Cooking Time ......... Temp......... Serves.........

## INGREDIENTS

## METHOD

## NOTES

# RECIPE FOR

Prep Time ......... Cooking Time ......... Temp......... Serves.........

## INGREDIENTS

## METHOD

## NOTES

# RECIPE FOR

Prep Time ......... Cooking Time ......... Temp. ......... Serves. .........

## INGREDIENTS

## METHOD

## NOTES

# RECIPE FOR

Prep Time ......... Cooking Time ......... Temp. ......... Serves. .........

## INGREDIENTS

## METHOD

## NOTES

# RECIPE FOR

Prep Time ......... Cooking Time ......... Temp. ......... Serves. .........

## INGREDIENTS

## METHOD

## NOTES

# RECIPE FOR

Prep Time ......... Cooking Time ......... Temp.......... Serves.........

## INGREDIENTS

## METHOD

## NOTES

# RECIPE FOR

Prep Time ......... Cooking Time ......... Temp. ......... Serves. .........

## INGREDIENTS

## METHOD

## NOTES

# RECIPE FOR

Prep Time ......... Cooking Time ......... Temp. ......... Serves. .........

## INGREDIENTS

## METHOD

## NOTES

# RECIPE FOR

Prep Time ......... Cooking Time ......... Temp......... Serves.........

## INGREDIENTS

## METHOD

## NOTES

# RECIPE FOR

Prep Time ......... Cooking Time ......... Temp .......... Serves..........

## INGREDIENTS

## METHOD

## NOTES

# RECIPE FOR

Prep Time ......... Cooking Time ......... Temp. ......... Serves. .........

## INGREDIENTS

## METHOD

## NOTES

# RECIPE FOR

Prep Time ......... Cooking Time ......... Temp......... Serves.........

## INGREDIENTS

## METHOD

## NOTES

# RECIPE FOR

Prep Time ......... Cooking Time ......... Temp. ......... Serves. .........

## INGREDIENTS

## METHOD

## NOTES

# RECIPE FOR

Prep Time ......... Cooking Time ......... Temp ......... Serves .........

## INGREDIENTS

## METHOD

## NOTES

# RECIPE FOR

Prep Time ......... Cooking Time ......... Temp. ......... Serves.........

## INGREDIENTS

## METHOD

## NOTES

# RECIPE FOR

Prep Time ......... Cooking Time ......... Temp ......... Serves .........

## INGREDIENTS

## METHOD

## NOTES

# RECIPE FOR

Prep Time ......... Cooking Time ......... Temp ......... Serves .........

## INGREDIENTS

## METHOD

## NOTES

# RECIPE FOR

Prep Time ........ Cooking Time ........ Temp. ........ Serves. ........

## INGREDIENTS

## METHOD

## NOTES

# RECIPE FOR

Prep Time ......... Cooking Time ......... Temp. ......... Serves.........

## INGREDIENTS

## METHOD

## NOTES

# RECIPE FOR

Prep Time ......... Cooking Time ......... Temp. ......... Serves.........

## INGREDIENTS

## METHOD

## NOTES

# RECIPE FOR

Prep Time ......... Cooking Time ......... Temp.......... Serves.........

## INGREDIENTS

## METHOD

## NOTES

# RECIPE FOR

Prep Time ......... Cooking Time ......... Temp. ......... Serves. .........

## INGREDIENTS

## METHOD

## NOTES

# RECIPE FOR

Prep Time ......... Cooking Time ......... Temp. ......... Serves. .........

## INGREDIENTS

## METHOD

## NOTES

# RECIPE FOR

Prep Time ......... Cooking Time ......... Temp.......... Serves.........

## INGREDIENTS

## METHOD

## NOTES

# RECIPE FOR

Prep Time ......... Cooking Time ......... Temp. ......... Serves.........

## INGREDIENTS

## METHOD

## NOTES

# RECIPE FOR

Prep Time ......... Cooking Time ......... Temp ......... Serves .........

## INGREDIENTS

## METHOD

## NOTES

# RECIPE FOR

Prep Time ......... Cooking Time ......... Temp. ......... Serves.........

## INGREDIENTS

| | | |
|---|---|---|
| ........................ | ........................ | ........................ |
| ........................ | ........................ | ........................ |
| ........................ | ........................ | ........................ |
| ........................ | ........................ | ........................ |
| ........................ | ........................ | ........................ |
| ........................ | ........................ | ........................ |

## METHOD

..........................................................................
..........................................................................
..........................................................................
..........................................................................
..........................................................................
..........................................................................
..........................................................................
..........................................................................
..........................................................................
..........................................................................
..........................................................................
..........................................................................
..........................................................................

## NOTES

..........................................................................
..........................................................................
..........................................................................

# RECIPE FOR

**Prep Time** ......... **Cooking Time** ......... **Temp** ......... **Serves** .........

## INGREDIENTS

## METHOD

## NOTES

# RECIPE FOR

Prep Time ......... Cooking Time ......... Temp. ......... Serves. .........

## INGREDIENTS

## METHOD

## NOTES

# RECIPE FOR

Prep Time ........ Cooking Time ........ Temp. ........ Serves. ........

## INGREDIENTS

## METHOD

## NOTES

# RECIPE FOR

Prep Time ......... Cooking Time ......... Temp. ......... Serves. .........

## INGREDIENTS

## METHOD

## NOTES

# RECIPE FOR

Prep Time ......... Cooking Time ......... Temp ......... Serves .........

## INGREDIENTS

## METHOD

## NOTES

# RECIPE FOR

Prep Time ......... Cooking Time ......... Temp. ......... Serves.........

## INGREDIENTS

## METHOD

## NOTES

# RECIPE FOR

Prep Time ......... Cooking Time ......... Temp. ......... Serves .........

## INGREDIENTS

## METHOD

## NOTES

# RECIPE FOR

Prep Time ......... Cooking Time ......... Temp. ......... Serves. .........

## INGREDIENTS

## METHOD

## NOTES

# RECIPE FOR

Prep Time ......... Cooking Time ......... Temp. ......... Serves. .........

## INGREDIENTS

## METHOD

## NOTES

# RECIPE FOR

Prep Time ......... Cooking Time ......... Temp. ......... Serves.........

## INGREDIENTS

## METHOD

## NOTES

# RECIPE FOR

Prep Time ......... Cooking Time ......... Temp. ......... Serves. .........

## INGREDIENTS

## METHOD

## NOTES

# RECIPE FOR

Prep Time ......... Cooking Time ......... Temp. ......... Serves.........

## INGREDIENTS

## METHOD

## NOTES

# RECIPE FOR

Prep Time ......... Cooking Time ......... Temp. ......... Serves. .........

## INGREDIENTS

## METHOD

## NOTES

# RECIPE FOR

Prep Time ......... Cooking Time ......... Temp. ......... Serves.........

## INGREDIENTS

## METHOD

## NOTES

# RECIPE FOR

Prep Time ......... Cooking Time ......... Temp. ......... Serves. .........

## INGREDIENTS

## METHOD

## NOTES

# RECIPE FOR

Prep Time ......... Cooking Time ......... Temp. ......... Serves.........

## INGREDIENTS

## METHOD

## NOTES

# RECIPE FOR

Prep Time ......... Cooking Time ......... Temp. ......... Serves. .........

## INGREDIENTS

## METHOD

## NOTES

# RECIPE FOR

Prep Time ......... Cooking Time ......... Temp. ......... Serves. .........

## INGREDIENTS

## METHOD

## NOTES

# RECIPE FOR

Prep Time ......... Cooking Time ......... Temp ......... Serves .........

## INGREDIENTS

## METHOD

## NOTES

# RECIPE FOR

Prep Time ......... Cooking Time ......... Temp......... Serves.........

## INGREDIENTS

## METHOD

## NOTES

# RECIPE FOR

Prep Time ......... Cooking Time ......... Temp. ......... Serves. .........

## INGREDIENTS

## METHOD

## NOTES

# RECIPE FOR

Prep Time ......... Cooking Time ......... Temp. ......... Serves. .........

## INGREDIENTS

## METHOD

## NOTES

# RECIPE FOR

Prep Time ......... Cooking Time ......... Temp. ......... Serves. .........

## INGREDIENTS

## METHOD

## NOTES

# RECIPE FOR

Prep Time ......... Cooking Time ......... Temp. ......... Serves.........

## INGREDIENTS

## METHOD

## NOTES

# RECIPE FOR

Prep Time ......... Cooking Time ......... Temp. ......... Serves.........

## INGREDIENTS

## METHOD

## NOTES

# RECIPE FOR

Prep Time ......... Cooking Time ......... Temp.......... Serves..........

## INGREDIENTS

## METHOD

## NOTES

# RECIPE FOR

Prep Time ......... Cooking Time ......... Temp. ......... Serves. .........

## INGREDIENTS

## METHOD

## NOTES

# RECIPE FOR

Prep Time ......... Cooking Time ......... Temp. ......... Serves. .........

## INGREDIENTS

## METHOD

## NOTES

# RECIPE FOR

Prep Time ......... Cooking Time ......... Temp. ......... Serves.........

## INGREDIENTS

## METHOD

## NOTES

# RECIPE FOR

Prep Time ......... Cooking Time ......... Temp......... Serves.........

## INGREDIENTS

## METHOD

## NOTES

# RECIPE FOR

Prep Time ......... Cooking Time ......... Temp. ......... Serves. .........

## INGREDIENTS

## METHOD

## NOTES

# RECIPE FOR

Prep Time ......... Cooking Time ......... Temp. ......... Serves. .........

## INGREDIENTS

## METHOD

## NOTES

# RECIPE FOR

Prep Time ......... Cooking Time ......... Temp. ......... Serves.........

## INGREDIENTS

## METHOD

## NOTES

# RECIPE FOR

Prep Time ......... Cooking Time ......... Temp. ......... Serves. .........

## INGREDIENTS

## METHOD

## NOTES

# RECIPE FOR

Prep Time ......... Cooking Time ......... Temp. ......... Serves. .........

## INGREDIENTS

## METHOD

## NOTES

# RECIPE FOR

Prep Time ......... Cooking Time ......... Temp. ......... Serves. .........

## INGREDIENTS

## METHOD

## NOTES

# RECIPE FOR

Prep Time ......... Cooking Time ......... Temp .......... Serves .........

## INGREDIENTS

## METHOD

## NOTES

# RECIPE FOR

Prep Time ......... Cooking Time ......... Temp. ......... Serves. .........

## INGREDIENTS

## METHOD

## NOTES

# RECIPE FOR

Prep Time ......... Cooking Time ......... Temp. ......... Serves. .........

## INGREDIENTS

## METHOD

## NOTES

# RECIPE FOR

Prep Time ......... Cooking Time ......... Temp. ......... Serves.........

## INGREDIENTS

## METHOD

## NOTES

# RECIPE FOR

Prep Time ........ Cooking Time ........ Temp. ........ Serves. ........

## INGREDIENTS

## METHOD

## NOTES

# RECIPE FOR

Prep Time ......... Cooking Time ......... Temp. ......... Serves. .........

## INGREDIENTS

## METHOD

## NOTES

# RECIPE FOR

Prep Time ......... Cooking Time ......... Temp. ......... Serves. .........

## INGREDIENTS

## METHOD

## NOTES

# RECIPE FOR

Prep Time ......... Cooking Time ......... Temp. ......... Serves.........

## INGREDIENTS

## METHOD

## NOTES

# RECIPE FOR

Prep Time ......... Cooking Time ......... Temp. ......... Serves .........

## INGREDIENTS

## METHOD

## NOTES

# RECIPE FOR

Prep Time ......... Cooking Time ......... Temp. ......... Serves. .........

## INGREDIENTS

## METHOD

## NOTES

# RECIPE FOR

Prep Time ......... Cooking Time ......... Temp. ......... Serves. .........

## INGREDIENTS

## METHOD

## NOTES

# RECIPE FOR

Prep Time ......... Cooking Time ......... Temp. ......... Serves. .........

## INGREDIENTS

## METHOD

## NOTES

# RECIPE FOR

Prep Time ........ Cooking Time ........ Temp. ........ Serves. ........

## INGREDIENTS

## METHOD

## NOTES

# RECIPE FOR

Prep Time ......... Cooking Time ......... Temp ......... Serves .........

## INGREDIENTS

## METHOD

## NOTES

# RECIPE FOR

Prep Time ......... Cooking Time ......... Temp. ......... Serves. .........

## INGREDIENTS

## METHOD

## NOTES

# RECIPE FOR

Prep Time ......... Cooking Time ......... Temp. ......... Serves. .........

## INGREDIENTS

## METHOD

## NOTES

# RECIPE FOR

Prep Time ........ Cooking Time ........ Temp. ........ Serves. ........

## INGREDIENTS

## METHOD

## NOTES

# RECIPE FOR

Prep Time ......... Cooking Time ......... Temp. ......... Serves. .........

## INGREDIENTS

## METHOD

## NOTES

# RECIPE FOR

Prep Time ......... Cooking Time ......... Temp. ......... Serves. .........

## INGREDIENTS

## METHOD

## NOTES

# RECIPE FOR

Prep Time ......... Cooking Time ......... Temp. ......... Serves. .........

## INGREDIENTS

## METHOD

## NOTES

# RECIPE FOR

Prep Time ........ Cooking Time ........ Temp. ........ Serves. ........

## INGREDIENTS

## METHOD

## NOTES

13992915R00057

Printed in Great Britain
by Amazon